# MANAGE MY EMOTIONS

*JUST FOR KIDS*

Kenneth Martz, Psy.D. & Meredith Martz

No part of this book may be reproduced in any form or by any means without the prior written permission of the publisher, except for brief quotes used in connection with reviews, written specifically for inclusion in a magazine or newspaper.

Warning – Disclaimer: The purpose of this book is to educate. This book is not intended to take the place of professional counseling. It is a tool to support anyone in their personal journey of growth. Consult your physician prior to beginning any physical exercise.

The author and/or publisher do not guarantee that anyone following these techniques, suggestions, tips, ideas or strategies will become successful. The author and/or publisher shall have neither liability nor responsibility to anyone with respect to any loss or damage caused, or alleged to be caused, directly or indirectly, by the information contained in this book.

### 1st Printing Edition, 2021

ISBN: 978-1-7357109-8-3 (print)

ISBN: 978-1-7357109-6-9 (digital)

www.DrKenMartz.com

Copyright © 2021 by Kenneth Martz

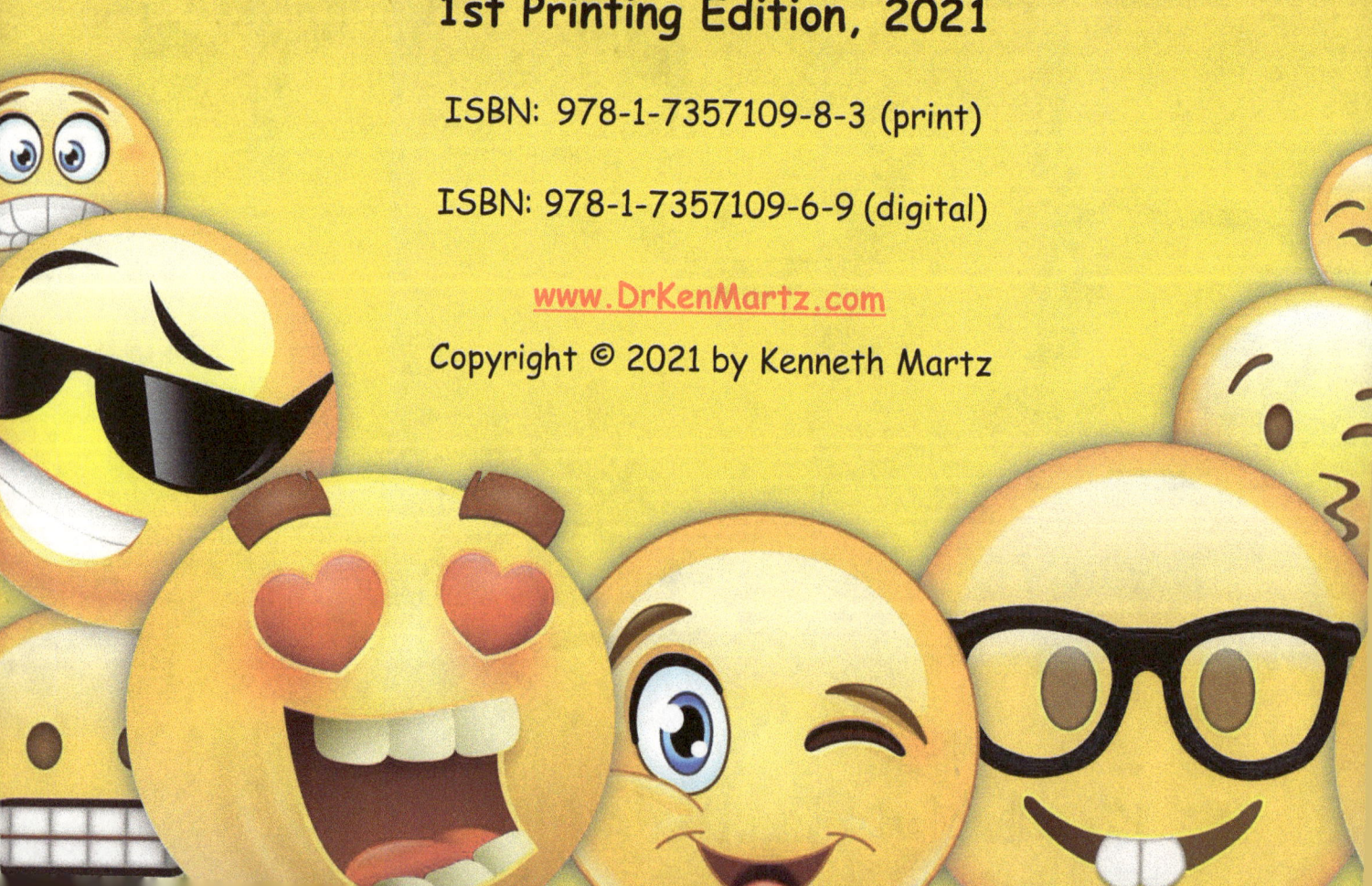

# To The Hope And Promise Of Our Next Generation

# Where Am I Now?

We all have a lot of different feelings. These can change quickly. Sometimes I am happy and at other times, I may be sad, mad, or scared.
Sometimes I can feel a bunch of feelings at once which can be confusing.

# The Role of Emotions

Feelings can help me.
When I am scared, it warns me of danger.
When I am mad, it lets me know I want something important.

When I feel upset there are
lots of things I can do.

Talk to someone close to me
Take three deep slow breaths
Play a game
Talk to a friend
Color or paint
Play outside
Do jumping jacks

What are two other things I like to do?

## Coping Skills

# Feelings and Emotions

When I am feeling mad or sad,
what is it like for me?

Where do I feel it in my body?
Is it in my head, face, or maybe
my chest or belly?

What does it feel like?
Is it heavy, light or maybe
even tight?

What do I do?
Do I make a fist or frown?

# Emotions and Learning

**When I practice anything, I will get better.**

When I practice, I will learn it more.
How can I practice being happy?

Tell a joke
Smile at someone
Play a game
Hug someone you love
Go on a playdate with a friend
Tell someone you trust two thing things you are thankful for

What are two other things I like to do?

# Awareness

## What am I feeling right now?
## (It is often more than one.)

# Practice

When I practice, I get better and stronger.

I can practice things to make me happy and proud by:

Making a list of important things
Repeating those things often.

# Courage and Fear

Do Superman or Wonder Woman get scared?
Courage is doing something even though we are scared.

I can practice by:

Standing tall, lifting my chest and putting my hands on my hips, and feeling strong like my favorite hero.
Imagining a big hug from someone who knows I can do it.
Remembering, "I am strong."

What is one other thing that helps me feel strong?

# Drive and Anger

**Is it OK to be angry?**

Yes. Anger means we know that we really want something important. ...And we still need to behave. No hitting or yelling.

When I am calmer, I can make better choices.

I can practice letting go of anger by:

Inhaling deeply. Then blow air out of my mouth very slowly, like blowing on hot food to cool it down. Every time I blow out air, I let the anger soften.

Doing some jumping jacks or physical activity for a few minutes.

What is one other thing that helps me feel calm?

# Joy and Boredom

Some days I get bored.

I can be creative!

I can draw
I can laugh
I can play a game
I can tell a joke
I can read a new book

What is one other thing that is fun to do?

# Compassion and Worry

Some days I worry.

I can practice being confident by:

Imagine a big hug from a helpful adult
Feel the Earth supporting me from below
Inhale and exhale slowly, feeling each breath

# Values and Sadness

When I value someone (or something), or love them a lot, I may feel sad or miss that person while they are away.

I can practice appreciation by:

Appreciating the things I have
Letting go of things I don't need
Cleaning my room
Writing a letter to the person I miss

## Play the Thankful Game
- Take turns with a friend
- Each person says one thing they are thankful for
- Go as fast as you can
- Get as many as you can

# Getting to Love

When I love someone, I may feel a lot of things.

I can practice helping the relationship:

- By helping clean up the dishes
- Playing games together
- Asking for help
- Giving warm hugs to the people I care about

# Communication

Asking and Listening are Very Important
I can practice communication by:
Asking for things that I want
Knowing that sometimes I don't get what I ask for
Listening for what others want
Helping others when I can

# Difficult Communication

Sometimes other kids say things that hurt.
Sometimes this is an accident.
Sometimes this is on purpose by a bully.
I can practice:
Keep my head up and shoulders back
Act brave and walk away without reacting
Remember I am strong
Talk to a helpful adult about it
Spend time with good friends

# Relationships

I get different emotions when I am with different people, like friends, teachers, brothers and sisters.

How quickly can I practice the things I've learned?

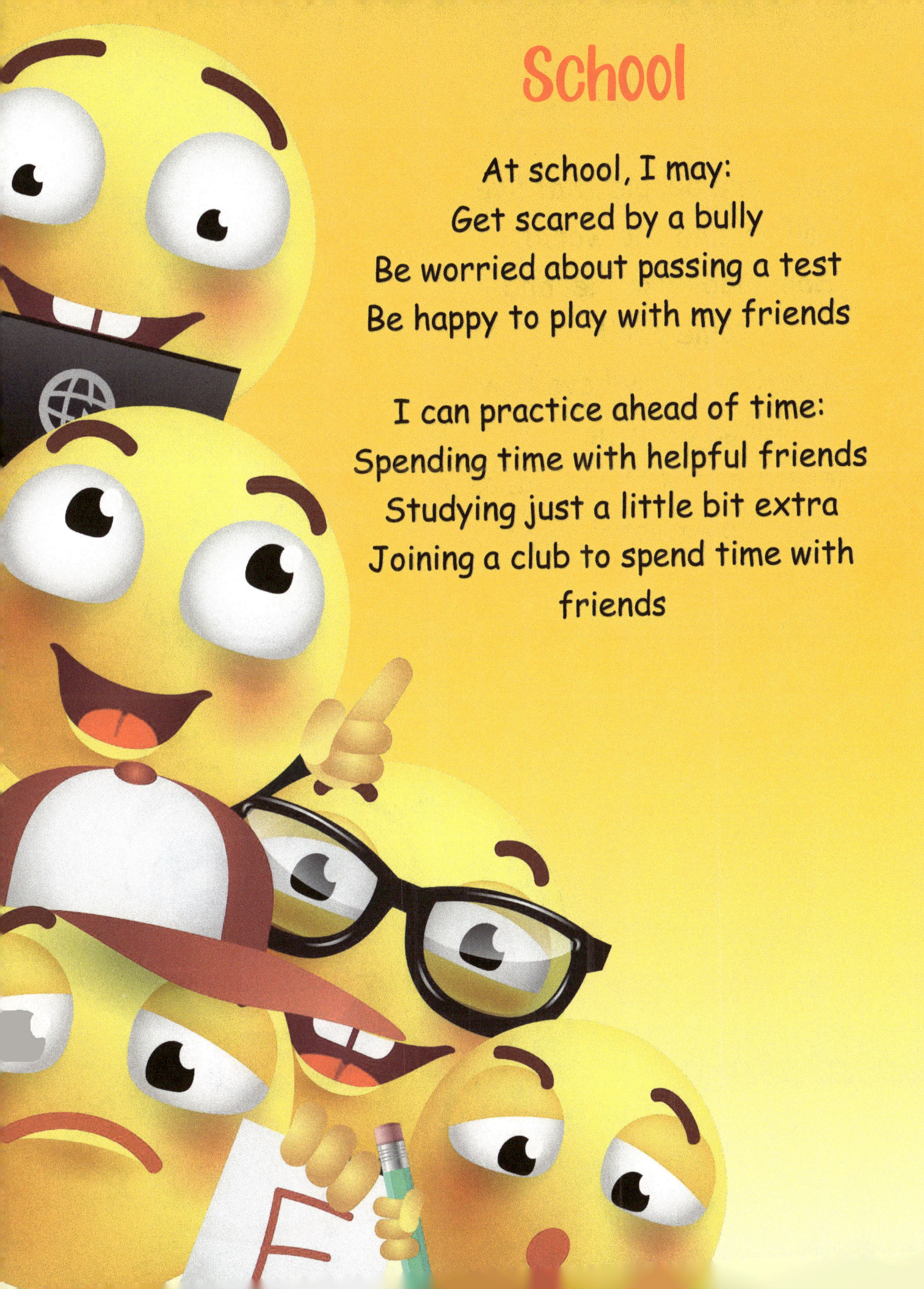

# School

At school, I may:
Get scared by a bully
Be worried about passing a test
Be happy to play with my friends

I can practice ahead of time:
Spending time with helpful friends
Studying just a little bit extra
Joining a club to spend time with friends

# Culture

There are people that live
all around the world.
Some look like me, and
some don't.
Sometimes they have new
ideas or games.
There are lots of new ideas
to explore!

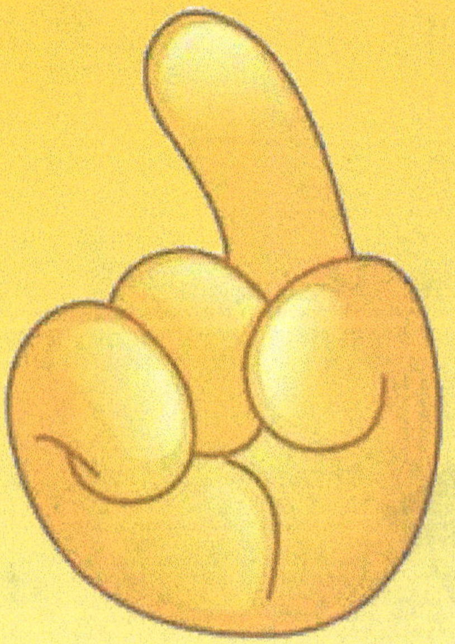

# Next Steps

**Remember and Repeat
These Words Often**

I am Strong

I am Friendly

I am Helpful

I am Worthy

I am Loved

I am Enough

My Mistakes Help Me Grow

The World Is a Safe Place

I Get Better Every Single Day

# About the Authors

Dr. Ken Martz is a licensed psychologist with more than 25 years experience. He is the bestselling author of <u>Manage My Emotions: What I Wish I'd Learned in School about Anger, Fear, and Love</u>

Meredith Martz is a high school student. She is an avid reader. She is also a member of the National Charity League, donating her time in community service to children and older adults in need.

Visit us to learn more and receive free resources at
<u>www.DrKenMartz.com</u>

# For Parents and Guardians

As a parent and educator, I want to emphasize the importance of emotional balance as a part of healthy growth and development.

This book may be read by a child alone or together with the parents.

Please visit our website to obtain a copy of the <u>Manage My Emotions Parent's Guide.</u> This free resource offers tips on how to begin conversations about emotions with your child and help to get the most out of this book.
You can access the download page directly through the link below.

<u>https://drkenmartz.com/mmek-request</u>

# Letting Go

A Mother's Gift to Her Child on Graduation Day

Copyright © 2017 by Dr. Sandra Saccucci Zaher, Ph.D.

All rights reserved. This book or any portion thereof may not be reproduced or used in any manner whatsoever without the express written permission of the publisher except for the use of brief quotations in a book review.

*To My Children, Nathan and Omar:*

*All the letters behind my name pale in comparison to one – M.O.M.*

*It is truly an honor to be your mom*

*All my love,*

*MML*

# Letting Go

A Mother's Gift to Her Child on Graduation Day

Dr. Sandra Saccucci Zaher, Ph.D.

Here we are, my angel, on this, your Graduation Day, a day marked by bittersweet dichotomies: laughter and tears; pride and yearning; loving and relinquishing. As I gaze at you in your cap and gown, I recall your birth day, and I know with every fiber of my soul, that letting go of you commenced on that very day. After all, the doctor did cut the umbilical cord, and thus severed our ties.

I know that loving you simultaneously means preparing *you* to let go of *me*. What I did not know until this day, is that loving you also means preparing *me* to let go of *you*. In a sense, your Graduation Day is also my Graduation Day because both of us have to forge a new path now; both of us have to re-define ourselves.

As I look at you today in your cap and gown, I know I'm supposed to see an adult face, but I don't: I see your baby face. In fact, I see a kaleidoscope of baby faces as I travel back in memory. I recall countless moments in time during which I tried to teach you life lessons, to prepare you for an independent life so that you could live well away from home – away from me.

*Can anything be more difficult than preparing your child to leave you?* But, that is, after all, the job.

I recall a particularly humorous moment when you were five years of age. It was bedtime and you didn't want to brush your teeth (as usual). I tried to convey to you the importance of oral hygiene. Your response was, "Mom, I feel a parent moment coming on." Well, sweetheart, think of this book as one L – O – N – G parent moment…

Insert Picture Here

_____
_____
_____
_____
_____
_____
_____
_____
_____

*A*LWAYS REMEMBER YOU at eight months old as you were learning to walk. I tried everything to no avail, and then one day, I held up an ice cream cone, and you not only walked, you practically sprinted for it! From that moment on, ice cream became your favorite food.

So, keep eating ice cream, my sweet angel. Keep experiencing simple joys.

www.ingramcontent.com/pod-product-compliance
Lightning Source LLC
Chambersburg PA
CBHW080627170426
43209CB00007B/1530

Insert Picture Here

_____
_____
_____
_____
_____
_____
_____
_____

WHEN YOU WERE three years of age, you and I filled your "little wallet" with photographs of people who love you: your father and I, siblings, grandparents, aunts, uncles, cousins and friends.

*Always keep your loved ones close to you. In a world which is often cold and heartless, those who love you will protect and warm you, even when they are not physically there with you.*

Insert Picture Here

*R*EAD. READ. READ. And don't "Ahhh mom me!" Reading will cultivate your intellect, enrich your perspective, and inspire your imagination. Imagination is the only true freedom in life because your imagination cannot be bound by any external boundaries, be they financial, physical or otherwise.

Insert Picture Here

*T*HINK HIGH, BUT *fly low*. The world is poisoned by jealousy. Those who achieve the most are most targeted. However, don't let jealousy thwart your achievements. Simply, stay guarded, but continue to strive. People will criticize you and try to destroy you, but continue anyway. People will throw unkind words and vicious rocks at you, but persist in walking down your own righteous path as you define it – with dignity and love in your heart. Love will protect you. Hate will destroy you.

Insert Picture Here

*K*EEP YOUR INNATE *sense of humour.* I recall many instances when you made me laugh. I recall a time when you were three years of age. I thought someone rang our doorbell and so you and I raced to the door. No one was there. I said, "Oh, it was a mistake." From then one, every time someone rang our doorbell, you would say, "Oh, it's Mr. Steak."

I also remember a comment you made when you were four years of age. You said, "Back in the olden days when I was three…" I laughed and laughed.

When you were five, you looked at me with those big, blue beautiful eyes and said, "Mommy, you're so tender." Of course, I stopped cooking and gave you a big bear hug. Then you asked me, "By the way, what does tender mean?" - always the charmer.

And what a charmer you were! I remember another time when you asked me, "When will your husband get home?" rather than "When will daddy get home?"

Humour will sustain and heal you as you embark on your journey up the mountain of life,
strive to reach its top,
and soar –
as I know you will.

Insert Picture Here

*F*ORGIVE THOSE WHO *hurt you*. This may very well be the hardest lesson you'll ever have to learn. Don't seek retribution or revenge because this will be like drinking a cup of poison yourself while expecting the other person to die. Hatred and hostility toward those who harm us are toxic, my beautiful child. Remember, forgiveness is not for those who harm us; forgiveness is for ourselves.

Insert Picture Here

*T*RUST YOUR DREAMS *and relinquish your fears to God, angel.* There will come a time when I will no longer be with you and only God will guide and protect you in my stead. Listen to your instincts for they are the whisperings of angels guiding you toward the path of integrity, honesty, community service and altruism.

Insert Picture Here

*V*ISIT THE LIBRARY *frequently.* This is an enchanted and magical world full of books with people who will inspire you, and teach you that the only thing in life standing between you and your goals is self-doubt.

Insert Picture Here

I REMEMBER YOUR "Terrible Twos" when your every response to anything I asked of you was a monosyllabic and emphatic "No!" Well, carry on with that response, my angel, only to drugs, alcohol and cigarettes. *Treat your body well and respect the mind-body connection.* As you develop your intellect, you may lose sight of one simple fact, simply because it is simple: your health is the single most important thing to you because without it, you cannot accomplish anything. In a nutshell, sweetheart, eat your vegetables!

Insert Picture Here

I REMEMBER ASKING you if you took care of your brother while I was out, to which you responded, "Yes, mom, I fed him; I watered him; and then I put him to bed." Children can make us laugh as no others.

*Love, love, love.* There is no greater bond than those rooted in childhood. Nurture and maintain your sibling relationships. Friends do come and go, but siblings remain for life. Remember, you can divorce a spouse, but you cannot divorce a sibling.

Insert Picture Here

R*EMAIN GENTLE.* I remember a time when you were six years of age and a child hit you at the school play ground. Your only response was, "No thank-you." The child was so disarmed he gave you his snack and you and he became best friends from that point onwards. Gentleness is a shield against aggression. You knew this instinctively as a child. Carry this gentleness into adulthood.

Insert Picture Here

YOU AND I used to celebrate Fridays evenings with popcorn and movies. I know you'll be carrying on this ritual with someone else now, and this knowledge both hurts and comforts me. *I want you to learn to take comfort in rituals because rituals not only add structure to life, they add substance.*

Insert Picture Here

_____
_____
_____
_____
_____
_____
_____
_____
_____

*S*ING LULLABIES TO *those you love.* One of the most beautiful tender moments I recall is you at the age of three singing a lullaby to your baby brother. I hope you preserve this tenderness and continue to use your voice to comfort, and not condemn. The world would be a better place if more men sung lullabies.

Insert Picture Here

I REMEMBER YOUR first day of school. You had a difficult time letting go as I dropped you off – a touch of separation anxiety. Now, as you embark on your post-secondary school education, I am certain you will experience the same feelings. I'll tell you now what I told you then: even though I'm not *with* you, I am still *within* you, in your heart, my love.

I'll let you in on a secret: parents also suffer separation anxiety when their children graduate and leave home. So, call us once and awhile because although you need and should fly, we need and should maintain your nest for you when you do decide to come home.

Insert Picture Here

ATTAIN THE BEST possible education, but remember education is not about power over others, it is about self-empowerment. Truly powerful people don't exert control over others; rather, they master self-control.

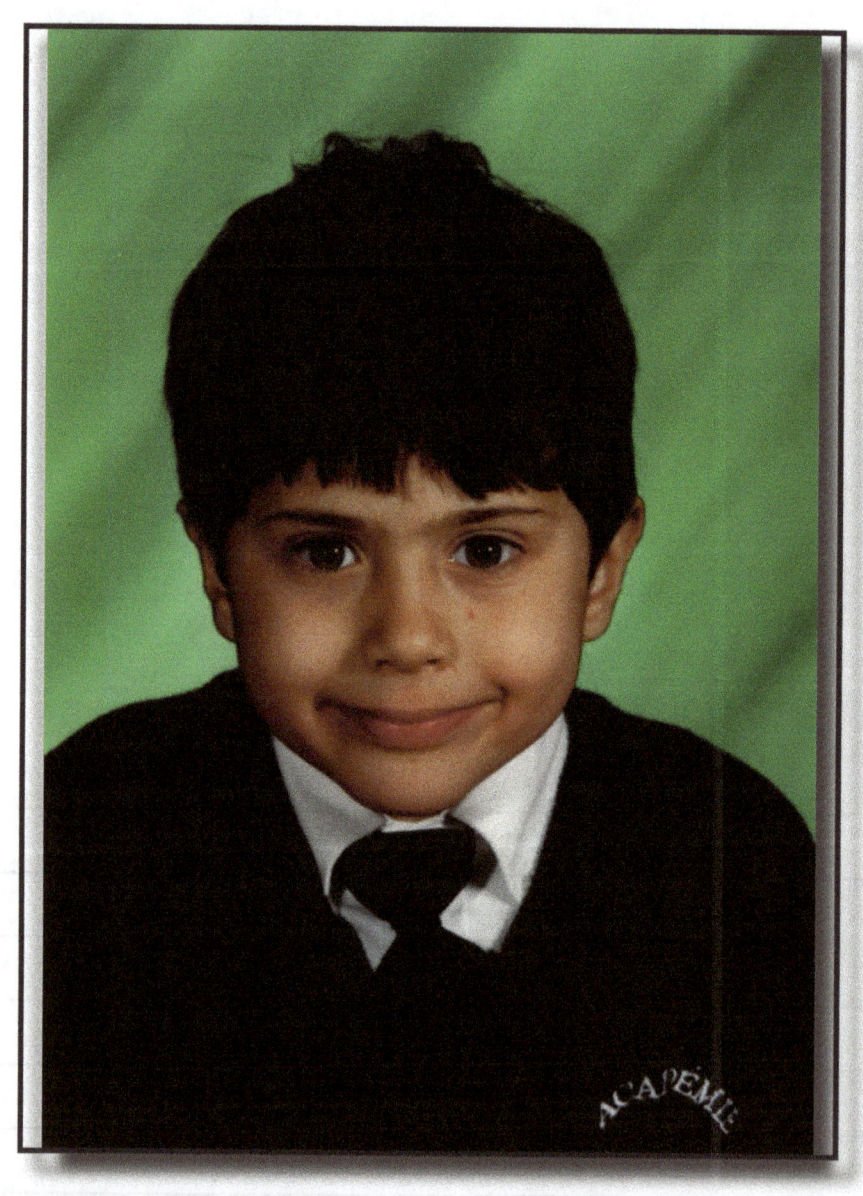

Insert Picture Here

I REMEMBER YOU asked me, "Mom, when we watch T.V. do the characters watch us too?" *Maintain this natural curiosity for this is precisely what fuels your drive toward education* Further, great inventions often begin with simple questions.

Insert Picture Here

And so, my angel, this is the day I have to let go of you, your Graduation Day. I have to let go so you can fly and reach your full potential, lofty goals and magical dreams. I gaze at you – as only a mother can or does – and I feel abysmally sad. I feel that I'm no longer your mother. You don't need me anymore. And then you turn to me and say, "Hey, mom, what's for dinner?" You don't even realize it, but this simple question is your gift to me because it is at that moment that I realize I am still a part of your life, and I always will be.

My last words to you are: don't follow in anyone's footsteps, not even your father's; rather, create your own footprints with the same passion you created your own snow angels when you were a child.

Insert Picture Here

_____
_____
_____
_____
_____
_____
_____
_____
_____

## ABOUT THE AUTHOR

DR. SANDRA SACCUCCI ZAHER earned her Doctorate from the University of Toronto, and went on to pursue a teaching career. She is a well published scholar and writer.

www.ingramcontent.com/pod-product-compliance
Lightning Source LLC
Chambersburg PA
CBHW080627170426
43209CB00007B/1531